Also by Stuart Dybek

Streets in Their Own Ink

Streets in Their Own Ink

Stuart Dybek

Farrar, Straus and Giroux / New York

Farrar, Straus and Giroux
19 Union Square West, New York 10003

Copyright © 2004 by Stuart Dybek
All rights reserved
Distributed in Canada by Douglas & McIntyre Ltd.
Printed in the United States of America
First edition, 2004

Library of Congress Cataloging-in-Publication Data
Dybek, Stuart, 1942–
    Streets in their own ink / Stuart Dybek.— 1st ed.
        p.   cm.
    ISBN-13: 978-0-374-27095-7
    ISBN-10: 0-374-27095-3 (alk. paper)
    1. City and town life—Poetry. I. Title.

PS3554.Y3S74 2004
813'.54—dc22

                                        2004043292

Designed by Jonathan D. Lippincott

www.fsgbooks.com

1   3   5   7   9   10   8   6   4   2

For Howard, Jane, and Emma

Quels sont les grands oublieurs
Qui donc saura nous faire oublier telle ou telle partie du monde
Où est le Christophe Colomb à qui l'on devra l'oubli d'un continent

Who are the great forgetters
Who will know just how to make us forget such and such a part
  of the world
Where is Christopher Columbus to whom is owed the forgetting
  of a continent

—Apollinaire, "Toujours"
(translated by Roger Shattuck)

Contents

I

Windy City

The garments worn in flying dreams
were fashioned there—
overcoats that swooped like kites,
scarves streaming like vapor trails,
gowns ballooning into spinnakers.

In a city like that one might sail
through life led by a runaway hat.
The young scattered in whatever directions
their wild hair pointed, and gusting
into one another, fell in love.

At night, wind rippled saxophones
that hung like wind chimes
in pawnshop windows, hooting through
each horn so that the streets seemed haunted,
not by nighthawks, but by doves.

Pinwheels whirred from steeples
in place of crosses. At the pinnacles
of public buildings, snagged underclothes—
the only flag—flapped majestically.
And when it came time to disappear

one simply chose a thoroughfare
devoid of memories, raised a collar,
and turned one's back on the wind.
I remember closing my eyes as I stepped
into a swirl of scuttling leaves.

Autobiography

1

Beneath the dripping udders
of tar paper roofs
a boy with a stolen jackknife
pries winter from spring.
That's how I'd begin,
with the smell of mud,
and icicles slipping into rain
as widows pass
unbalanced between shopping bags,
lugging mysterious griefs
by the scruff to novenas.

2

Our Lady of Sorrows,
the Black Virgin of Czestochowa,
was my girlfriend.
Once, while praying,
I saw her smile.
Any old woman
palsied with love and terror
I called *babushka*.
No word in English turns
a scarf into a grandmother.

3

And every morning was a requiem
or the feast day of a martyr—
the priest in red or black,
cortege of traffic, headlights
funneling through incense
under viaducts. While my surplice
settled around me like smoke
my father rode the blue spark
of a streetcar to the foundry
where, in the dark mornings,
the cracks of carbonized windows
flowed with the blood of stained glass.

4

Actually, by noon
the streets were ordinary—
lampposts, sparrows, sewers—
but we knew behind the light
there were other streets
transfigured by a reverence
I can't explain, where
hoodlums stood hooded in violet
like statues in Lent,
and whores were blue
from kissing police.

5

There were autobiographies
at every corner,
legends, litanies, manifestos,
memoirs in forgotten tongues,
h a silent hiss
in every *t'anks*.
Autobiographies, but no history,
and by the clang of evening Angelus
the babble condensed into a drone
murmured behind a jukebox sax
tailing from an open bar.

6

When it rained on Eighteenth Street
I believed that rain was falling
all over the world. I believed
the neighborhood's war dead were buried
beneath the plaque of their names
on the corner Victory garden,
and I worried that if people kept dying
the earth would be used up for cemeteries.
I worried that if we kept using
the same notes over
we'd run out of songs.

7

As one grows up into rebellion,
the dead slowly vanish.
Later, perhaps, they reappear.
Sometimes, I'd still catch glimpses
of that parish of phantoms
childhood borders—spirits
locked in a mazurka with a crucifix,
rumors expelled from a confessional,
wading a gutter under streetlights
as if blood, instead of April muck,
swirled around their black galoshes.

8

I've left out nothing;
these images are what I learned.
It's not that I didn't listen,
but it wasn't my language
in matters of sex or money.
What might have been told
was abandoned like excess baggage,
and the commonplace has assumed
the mysterious presence
of the lost.

9

What I finally remember is feeling
free. That's how I'd end, walking off
into an epilogue of the present
where allegiance is pledged to dream
rather than to tarnished emblems
of memory. Its flag of wind snaps
over a republic stoked by the energy
required to forget continents.
Each personal revolution equal
in a mass migration out of history.
Each step, a further separation;
my story, another voice receding
behind the solo of a saxophone
noodling through broken English.

Bath

She mops a washcloth down his spine and scrubs
until his bones glow with the inner light of porcelain
and when his Haloed hair bursts into foam
he holds his nose and dunks beneath the soapy gloom
ears flooding with signals
the pipes transmit like microphones.

The boy can hear another city, the one below
where wind coils when it isn't howling,
can hear Purgatory boil
up through the manholes, a river flushing souls
into the underworld, tomorrow's news
bawled at the crossroad of subway and sewer.

If he were accidentally to swallow here
the water would taste like silver
off a dead man's eyes. Upstairs,
the mute émigré waitress he secretly
adores sings naked in the shower,
the newlyweds from Mexico

rage about *dinero*, next door
a newborn wails like a Black Maria,
while in a hidden room, a crazy old man
won't stop repeating "the goddamn, the goddamn!"
And then the boy comes up for air,
eyes burning, rinsed hair silky, his hands
wrinkled, *Busha* says, as prunes.

Overhead, the bare bulb fogs with steam.
She jerks the plug, the drain

gulps a vortex of gray bathwater.
It's time to rise before it sucks him down,
to stand calf-deep, lacquered with Ivory,
smoldering before a faucet that trickles

a cool stream at which *Busha* washes him
first gently in front and then behind
in a way that no one else will ever wash him.
The moon, too, must be fogged above
misted lamps that bleed into reflections
on the marbled pane.

He swipes abstractions in the sweat,
finger painting night
while *Busha* towels his hair
as if reviving a drowned sailor
the sea has graciously returned.
Don't worry, *Busha*, your grandson is clean

for Saturday night:
ears, navel, nails, inspected,
teeth unstained, cleansed as baptism
leaves the soul, pure enough to sleep—
as you instruct him—with the angels,
cleaner than he'll ever be again.

The Volcano

It rose from an industrial wasteland
at the end of the block
and loomed over the neighborhood,
but only at night were its true dimensions
visible: a mountain of darkness,
its cone consumed from within
like a coal, porous with seismic tunnels
leaking searchlights, magma stoked
behind blackened, vandalized windows,
the night shift in the caldera
burning off spirit in updrafts
of sparks, the smudged moon a cinder
adrift in plumes of chimney smaze.
To those below, born in its shadow,
ash was the natural smell of air.
They thought its tremors were their own
suppressed emotions, its molten
eruptions the lust night drew
from their bodies. They never noticed,
come morning, how they'd been recast
going about their daily routines:
a butcher, his cleaver hacked
into igneous lamb; an old babushka
who'd stooped to pick fairy rings
on her way to mass. There,
a woman hanging stone sheets;
here, a man caught in the flow
just as he'd raised a hand
to strike his son
or brush the hair from his eyes.

The Sunken Garden

Over a back-alley fence woven from morning
glory vines I'd drop into a sunken garden
behind the sinking bungalow of a witch
from Warsaw who'd been displaced
to an asylum on Twenty-third, hidden in foliage.
The efflorescence was what was foreign.
I've forgotten my recurrent dreams
set there, except for one in which I lived
in a hutch with a wild rabbit.
When I woke that winter morning for school,
I left him behind, although I continued to hope
that some night, across the border of sleep,
we'd meet again. Alley cats
barely survived our neighborhood,
and I never saw a rabbit in her garden,
but there were yellow birds—finches, probably—
I thought of as a gang of caged canaries
escaped into the wild, twittering with freedom
as if tuned to her orchestra of wind chimes.
Swallowtails hovered on the updrafts
of their shadows. It was a workers' paradise
for bees. I'd catch them in snapdragons
and cradle the furiously buzzing blossoms
for blocks, back to our flat, to throw
at my younger brother. I'd like to think
it was my way of bringing him flowers.

Fish Camp

In the Coleman's glassy glare
my brother's switchblade
unriddles backlash. A bullhead,
the weight of a rat,
flops in the dirt, dropped
when its spine added a scar
to the lines of my palm.
Bullheads should utter some cry.
Someone should have warned
those city boys, fishing at night
on the shore of a dump,
how gills, drowning in air, gape
like wounds that won't heal;
someone should have taught them
how to kill and properly gut
what they lured out of darkness.

Benediction

The fly is giving another sermon;
we bow to mud, receiving absolution from a worm.
Impatient with the pace of prayer
—the journey's too long to make on our knees—
we scour the alleys for discarded slogans,
for proverbs banned from Bibles,
ignited by guitars—electric fire
branding air with a graffiti of psalms.

My clothesline whip drove wind and stars;
pigeons, not ponies, pulled my droshky.
At dusk, we traced the peddler's dirge
to the misted mouth
of a viaduct that swallowed full moons.
The horizon was strung on the other side,
but when a border of boxcars rumbled its drums
we fled down the neon tail
of the comet known as Cermak Road.

Night was that narrow—
a strip of darkness between shop signs.
Snow fell from the height
of a streetlamp.
I knew the names of seven attending angels
but was seventeen before I saw
my first jay.

Yet I worshipped the natural world
like an immigrant
in an adopted country—
the one in which he should have been born.

For me, the complexity of a grasshopper
catapulting
from the Congo behind a billboard
was irrefutable proof
of God and his baffling order.
And in my heart
I still kneel on a weed lot in summer,
seeking benediction
beneath the glittering cross
of a dragonfly.

Ginny's Basement

A green light filtered
through the morning glory vines
that twined through rusty screens
against sooty little panes
of windows level with the weeds.
We were deeper than the tulip bulbs
glowing under flower beds,
than the tangled roots of zinnias,
forget-me-nots, and hollyhocks
that hung their heads
beneath a noon sun
native to her wild backyard.

Down crumbling steps
mortared with moss,
we'd descended
from summer's feverish perfume
to the cool damp reek of drains,
from the tweet of flirting songbirds
and torqued thrum of bees
to the nasal echoes
of underground mains
toward which startled water bugs
scurried.

There was an odor of shadow
and cats, of moldering lint,
a sneezy scent of spilled detergent—
blue trails of Fab
that led to a wringer wash machine
gagged on a bedspread.

The furnace door stood open
like a tabernacle looted of flame.
The low, unfinished ceiling
required that we bow

beneath its canopy
of clothesline and live wires
snubbed in electric tape.
A necklace of cold sweat
beaded from tarnished pipes.
At a workbench, a vise
clenched a sawed strip of molding.
I tried to erase
the prints my sneakers
tracked through sawdust.

Deeper than they plant the dead,
beneath windows veined
with morning glory vines,
a ledge of pickle jars
filled with bolts and washers
reflected, like dusty concave mirrors,
the flash of skin
as her unbuttoned sundress fell
to the cobwebbed case of empties
at the base of her spine.

Mowing

for Dennis Zacek

A menial labor is reserved for the minority
called boys: sun bull's-eyed on his back,
he's dragged until he has to shove
as the squealing blade rages into hummocks
and chokes out dust. He's mowing an alley
through ragweed and cornflowers
in an overgrown valley behind a billboard.
At a dollar below minimum wage,
if they want him to devour the stunted wilderness
that sprouts behind a Camel ad, he will
because he's sure they don't remember
where one can still find a real snake
in this city. They don't recall,
if they ever knew, the secret location
of the junked backcountry of youth
where sanctuaries of jackrabbits
and songbirds survive along flyways
of rusted tracks, and the twittering prairie,
in view of downtown's smoggy range
of spires, basks in summer
behind the chain link of bankrupt factories.
There, once, down by the Sanitary Canal,
a fox like a four-legged fire
flashed across his incredulous eyes,
a fox trotting the edge of a marsh
unmarked on any street map,
three blocks from the thunder
of semis on the Stevenson overpass,
a limp rat dangling from its jaws.

Christening

Snow fell as it had all night,
and from the look of the drifts he waded
he was the first one out on Twenty-fourth Street.
Dragging a sack of newspapers
that erased his footprints, he became
aware of a sound barely audible
above the hiss of canvas. Strange birds,
too luminous for winter cities,
chirred from the maple along his route,
a tree he'd watched rust scarlet,
then fade to the shade of overripe pears.
Its matted leaves were now inscribed
with the hieroglyphics of bird tracks.
A synchronized wingbeat and the flock
gusted into a syllable and vanished,
a cry less to do with language
than the vocalization of snow,
its meaning a music hidden from words,
a farewell, perhaps, but he'll remember
hearing—years before he heard
from his own mouth, smothered by her hand—
the first wild gasp of her name.

Narcissus

Down on his hands and knees
outside the biker bar
as if searching the pavement
for his tooth; between the kick
that lacerated a kidney,
and the kick that cracked a rib,
my ex-pug uncle, Chino,
said he caught a look
he hadn't seen for years
on the distorted face
that lovingly gazed back at him
from a blood-spattered hubcap.

Boundary

It traces the irregularities of pavement,
fills cracks, floods the gaps
planned for expansion in the heat,
eddies into a sticky ring beneath
a pop bottle, before pooling
in the gutter, the way an eye socket
pools, until every aspect of the street
is soaked in a stretch of shade
noon can't erase, wine dark,
a birthmark the chalked outline
of a body can't contain.

It fades as it flowed, gradually,
but in summer's bleaching brightness,
beneath a shrill of blackbirds,
children moving to the beat
of the outraged boombox they shoulder
drop their voices as they pass
through the shadow, and the basketball
trotting beside them balks
at the border of the stain.

Shoesa

At the wake, the boy noticed that his uncle
Chino was to be buried without his *shoesa*.
Socks, underwear, trousers, whatever else
his uncle wore was said in English.
But for some reason, now forever undisclosed,
he used broken Polish for his shoes.
And the boy and his younger brother
had coined their own secret name
for their uncle's *shoesa*, too: Wino Shoes.
Puke on them and they want to prance
through dogshit. Laces snapped, they keep
trudging over miles of broken whiskey bottles
like a barefoot true believer over coals.
They'll lead down a street of shadowboxers
where no one asks, "Shine?"
Tongues panting, holey soles, those down-
at-heels, gimpy, scuffed limpers were perfect
for the coming dance craze, the Blind Staggers.
Probably when they tried to stuff them
into the coffin, somebody joked, "Yo,
watch it! They might kick!"
Yeah, but only against themselves.

Chord

A man steps out of sunlight,
sunlight that streams like grace,

still gaping at blue sky
staked across the emptiness of space,

into a history where shadows
assume a human face.

A man slips into silence
that began as a cry,

still trailing music
although reduced to the sigh

of an accordion
as it folds into its case.

Election Day

Though decked out in the Stars and Stripes,
the polling place was still a funeral home,
but then, ours was a precinct of funeral homes,
the way some neighborhoods are known
for their shoe stores or butcher shops.
On Election Day, the usually phantasmal aldermen
were out shaking hands, dressed in black
cashmere overcoats like proper mourners.
The air smelled of cigars and bars
and incense from the church whose doors
stood open as if at any moment
a coffin might come barging into traffic.
A cortege of dark Caddies lined the tow zones.
It might be a deceptive day with two-party weather:
one side of the street, Indian Summer,
December on the other, especially when wind
muscled the shadows that gathered as if the dead
were lurking—lost souls, spirits wandering
like drunks wondering where they'd parked
their cars, ghosts—most of them still voting.

Angelus

It's the metallic hour
when birds lose perfect pitch.
On a porch, three stories up,
against a copper window
facing the El,
a woman in a satin slip
and the geraniums she waters
turn to gold.

Beneath the street the blue clapper
of a switch swings in the tunnel.
Blocks away, a crescendo is overtaken
by its echo, and the reverberation
passes among strangers.
Shadows quiver like sheet metal.
High heels pace off down a platform
like one hand on a piano.

There's a note struck every evening—
every evening held longer—
a clang only because it's surrounded by silence,
chimes of small change
from the newsstand, trousers
full of keys and coins
flopped on a chair beside the bed,
the tink of bracelets
as her arm sweeps back her hair.

II

Sirens

Tonight they seem to be calling
from afar, conversing
like chained dogs carrying on an argument
from blocks away;

open windows still gasping from the night before,
and yet a fire truck screams more flame,
while the warning of an ambulance ricochets
across the carats of dark panes.

A network of stained crazing
like the backside of the moon
spreads beneath tea leaves, through a china cup
in which the future is contained,

but would the Black Maria be allowed
if its soprano struck the perfect pitch of glass,
if its aria were graphed
by a crack traveling the luminous city

reflected along the cliffs of the Gold Coast?
As dreamers know, it's possible
to rush in silence toward disaster
the way one rushes toward desire.

Current

The third rail
and the electric chair

are charged with the current
that glows tonight

in the bedside lamp
illuminating your body.

Swan

Amid the fifties bric-a-brac
in my mother's museum
of a shadow box mirror—

a blue Madonna blessed in Rome,
an Alpine village in a globe
that snowed when turned upside down,

and a miniature piano
with a key that unlocked Chopin—
there lived a swan

that could change even the doily
upon which it swam
into a crystalline pond.

Daylight fresh from your body;
what's most lovely about you
is elusive: light projected

through a glass figurine,
magnified into a refraction
brighter than substance,

a prismatic shadow
that transforms
whatever object it surrounds.

Seven Sentences

One
Tonight, the moon has a street number.

Jasmine
The darkness is scented like a love letter, too sweet, as if we've stepped into the wake left by girls in my old neighborhood before they learned to go easy on their heart-shaped vials of dime-store perfume.

Breath:
a concertina of evening air pressed back and forth between us in a doorway.

Proverb
"Old age is no joy; death is no wedding" was my grandmother's favorite proverb, though it rings right only as she would say it, in Polish: "*Starość nie radość . . .*"

Perspective
There's a perspective to a sentence and within its order a trail of discarded clothes leading beyond the frame.

A Novel
In freshman year at college I bought a used copy of John Updike's novel *Rabbit Run*, and there's a single sentence from it that I've never forgotten, perhaps in part because whoever owned the book before me had underlined in blue ink *He slid from her like sand.*

Seven
It will take more than a new day to erase tonight's moon.

Sleepers

A sleeper
purifies a room.

With each inhalation
the bed rises higher,

with each exhalation
less dust,
more perfection.

A vigil light
reflects through bone,

sleep coats
the slightest irritant
with nacre.

Now, in a counter-
levitation, the bed
is sinking into earth.

The sleepers pull their roofs down
for a quilt.

With every breath the moon
swells brighter,

their nakedness
begins to flower,

ferns leave imprints
on their skin.

Kitty-Corner

I'd like to call you long distance,
but even the Platonic form
for phone booth has been gutted;

besides, you only live downstairs
in the basement of an evening gown.

I wanted to say that last night
was the cross between a novena
and a rummage sale.

Instead, I'm wondering
how they could abolish the Public Phone.
It was so fragile,

a Japanese lantern swaying on a corner
jingling dimes in a hatch of moths,

a neon wafer dissolving in snow
to hardly anything, your voice,
frost around a bullet hole.

What will go next?
The newspaper kiosk kitty-corner
from the phone booth?

What will become of its burning
trash can and blind vendor?
What will become of us?

Night Walk

A light beneath the pavement
slaps against your soles;

in each doorway
a cat preaches sleep.

Despite the same scuffed moon
bolted at each corner to a listing pole,

each intersection offers
a new start. Pass by

the alleys mazing toward dead ends
where tarpaulins flap

without a breath of wind,
avoid the side streets dim

with misty haloes. Perhaps
an Angel of Mercy presides tonight,

guarding the crossroads, guiding
choices we make with each heartbeat,

and yet, if mercy is required,
isn't it already too late?

Remember, one shoe must step
before the other;

don't lag behind
the stride of your shadow;

the rule on city nights
is still: keep moving.

The Estrangement of Luis Leon

Luis Leon
cuts adrift

sinks flies
flickers out

it's dark
in his room

they screw
in a bulb

find rags
on hangers

resembling
his body

a pinup
with a thumbtack
stigmata

crucifix
with a snapped
G-string

scars that precede
the wounds
that caused them

an invisible nation
tattooed
on an abandoned
shadow

rattrap
abandoned

abandoned mirror
blued by the wind
of a muzzle

desire abandoned
anger abandoned

birth death
abandoned abandoned

cortege of roaches
carting off crumbs

in other words
nothing

much changed
by his absence

loans outstanding
love

and other debts
still outstanding

Don't worry kids
you still have
twelve uncles

and children are born
to mourn lost fathers

Don't worry Mother
you aren't blind
nobody sees him

Curtains

Sometimes they are the only thing beautiful
about a hotel.
Like transients,
come winter they have a way of disappearing,
disguised as dirty light,
limp beside a puttied pane.
Then some April afternoon
a roomer jacks a window open,
a breeze intrudes,
resuscitates memory,
and suddenly they want to fly,
while men,
looking up from the street,
are deceived a moment
into thinking
a girl in an upper story
is waving.

Three Windows

The first was painted stuck
many times over,
each time a fresh color.

The ropes of the second were frayed,
weights lost in the sash.
It must have crashed like a guillotine
and they replaced the pane
with cardboard.

The third opened opposite a wall.
Whoever lived here
left on the sill, beside the ashtray
of a seashell, burnt matchsticks
in the shape of a man, his erect penis
the length of his arms and legs.

Maja

Left breast swollen double
the size of its flabby twin, nipples—
tips of melted plastic—a scar
from what might have been a botched
vivisection, transversed
on her distended belly by a pink
impression of elastic, and when,
as directed, she rolls over
in the yellowed bedsheet: boils.

He's posed her amid mottled sunbeams
on a mattress stained with rust
or blood, before a shadeless window
that if not opaque with dust
would look out on the street
once known as Skid Row. Except
for a pervert with a Polaroid, years ago,
this is the first time anyone
has paid to take her picture.

He gauges light, asks her to *recline*—
his word—then ducks behind a tripod,
explaining that all he wants from her
is simply to pretend he isn't there.
She lights a smoke, exhales,
the shutter clicks, she smiles
as if to show she still has teeth,
licks her lips, adjusts her hair.
"Please," he says, "I want it natural."

The last artist simply wanted
to beat her up, which explains
placating the lens as if it were
a muzzle. She knows the danger
isn't that he's aiming at her soul
but that, thanks to dumb luck—
blind chance posing as salvation—
she's survived beyond a point
when anyone in his right mind
would pay for her to simply fuck.

View

Across from the hotel,
which had advertised a view,
a building was being dismantled.

She undressed looking out
to where a wall had been torn down
so that rooms revealed their entrails
of pipes and wires,

their secret memories, desires,
and paltry souls of peeling paint.
Just think, she said,

unzipping her skirt, of all
the lovemaking that happened there.
Just think of all the broken hearts,
she said, as her bra fell.

Journal

In a dream journal kept as an experiment,
evidence of a life that went
on without him while he slept, salvaged
fragments that might yield revelations
about the past or future, he found himself
recording nights they spent together.

On a page of frozen landscape
across which he towed his father,
now shrunk into a child, on a sled
meant to transport a dead battery,
was the August night she'd wiped
their sweat with unbound hair.

Rowing a turbulent sea of doors
he woke to a tingle of wings, a bat
brushing the wind chime in her room,
and hovering lips alighting along
the length of his body. He was lost
on a shore where clarinets were

driftwood, and sunrise a camisole
slipped from a shoulder. Each time
she came, she cried; erect nipples
tasting of tears, earlobes familiar
with their taste of pearls.
The mortgage on his soul was down

to a dollar, but where to pay it off?
Baby, she said, we're practicing
kissing interruptus. To save the world
from humankind, a desperate cabal
of cetaceans merged the psychic power
of their enormous brains.

His handprint still emblazoned
on her ass as she stepped into the shower.
Prisoners of war, assigned a classroom
in which to await decapitation,
sat passively at fifth-grade desks
while he paced, wishing for a gun,

and when the executioners rushed in,
it was another night in which the choice
was death or starting from the dream.
3 a.m. He lay listening to her breath,
wondering should he gently wake her
with his tongue, or let her sleep.

Three Nocturnes

1
Imperfect dreams,
each sleeper hung

on the meat hook
of a question mark,

clocks stuck
on an hour

when loneliness
seems just another

way of loving
only yourself.

What's the plural of dark?
Nighthawks

reciting a thousand names
for night,

a moon
you'd have to sort

through thousands of streetlights
to find.

2
An impression of her body
left tangled in sheets

patterned with moonlit craters
by the lace curtain

that had printed her back
with sprays of wildflowers

native, perhaps, to a field
in southern Bohemia.

And, beyond the field,
through an open window,

a moonlit river
that, despite its pessimism,

mirrors swans.
Or so the bed, abandoned,

was dreaming on its own.
I wouldn't sleep there,

I wouldn't kneel and pray
beside it.

3   *for John Woods, 1926–1995*
Pizzicato of wings
against screens . . . Listen to the roar

of weed lots, or the wilds
behind illuminated billboards

where shadows of nighthawks soar
across enormous faces. You'll hear

a hunger that can't be satisfied
in an all-night diner.

Night flyers won't let night stall.
Wingbeats fan darkness

as if it were a flame
able to flare up darker still.

In phosphorescent headlights,
projected moths

in which the moon is visible
unfurl from cocoons of oblivion;

time metamorphoses
into a perfume of black marigolds.

Nylon

She sends a nylon,
black, perfumed,
a shadow
of a slender leg

that he can fold
inside a pocket
or bury in a drawer
(hidden like a mask

he might wear
to rob a bank)
that he can crush
into a ball

and hurl into the sky
(then watch
while outer space
floats back

to his face)
that he can trace
along his lips
or slide

up his own thigh
or slip into a knot
that slowly tightens
at his throat.

Vigil

On a brick street slicked
with a ruby, numinous neon,
I thought I saw you again,
bareheaded in damp weather.
I recognized the shape
of your breath in the cold.
To whom else could that shadow belong
when, by the flickered vigil light
of bums cupping a match
in radiant hands, you passed?
From the all-night laundromat
the great round sloshy eyes
of wash machines watched
through steamed windows.
With each rap of your heels,
your legs, distorted but still
beautiful, disappeared
down a chrome aisle of hubcaps,
and raising my arm, I remembered
the weight of your body
reflected along the length
of a silver-plated cuff link
cloudy with sweat.

III

Vespers

Wearing a surplice of billowing curtains
an altar boy kneels ringing a bell
at the shoreline of an undertow.
A black umbrella opens with an angry blow

bruising the underside of clouds.
Rain stirs backyards to broth.
A barrow of soup bones sets off
like a blood clot late for a stroke.

Above back-alley roofs, stalagmites of spires
vanish, dismantled
                                        from bottom up by fog—
                    a labor of aeons erased in an afternoon.

Through the cracked, lampblacked spectacles
of a cellar window,
                                        poisonous pulpits,
                        erected by drizzle, ascend.

We ran beside the carriage,
a rusted shopping cart whose sole passenger stood
　　regal as a queen in rags
　　　　on her way to the guillotine;

　　she blessed the spitting rabble
　　while to the rap of a snare
a somber procession of blackbirds
brought up the rear,
　　　　　　　wings
　clasped like wringing hands behind their backs,
　　　pausing only to bow

　　　　to undigested seeds
　　　　　of grass
　　　in steaming pats of manure.

What was the record wingspan for a crucified Christ?
Maybe in the old Polish church on Ashland:
they didn't have a Black Madonna who wept
real tears like a doll, or a sister
with the stigmata, but their Son
with his long sinewy arms
ending in the punctuation of nailed palms,
was second to none. By the flicker
of vigil candles, he seemed to take flight.
In the glow of the sanctuary lamp
his wounds were varying reflections of red,
as if his bare, agonized body had been kissed
by different shades of lipstick.
Once, when I thought I was in love,
I was sure I recognized the imprint of her lips
on the wounds of his feet.

Beneath a daylight moon, the bag lady
kids called the Hag
foraged doubled beneath the hump
she lugged everywhere.

Were she the Goddess of the Hunt,
forever young, lithe as a bow, half bare,
the gilded fall of her undone chignon
would have made nakedness demure.

Instead, a matted gray flow (the grotesque
can take the length of a life to grow)
swept the pavement before her every step.

A dog pack ran, further clearing the way.
Her battered straw purse proudly swung
from the mouth of a dirty white hound.

In a room the sepia of sunset-beaten shades,
she was wearing only pearls;
anointed with sweat, her girlish body
straddled his as if they were riding.
The pearls whipped them to a furious pace
until she snatched her necklace out of air
and held it in her mouth, and he could hear
the sound of their bodies colliding
mimicked by the sound her lips made
as one by one she sucked the pearls
against her tongue (the way an old nun,
he unaccountably remembered, blissfully
fingered each blessed bead) and then
a hail as she bit down.

After they report their own absence
to the Department of Missing Persons,
and the crime of nostalgia
seems the only defense against amnesia,
it's to this street that prodigals come
to live out those final days before
they are reduced to seeking forgiveness.

One last nuzzle against the shoulder of night
along which stars are sprinkled with the disorder
of freckles beneath a bra strap.
Soon enough the sailors float home
from around the block, facedown
through the old neighborhoods that lie below
a sea of flooded basements.

What's all this suffering for, Father?
Nothing, my Son . . . the same as all this love.

I tried to pay
for a link of sausage
with a rosary

snarled in what I'd thought
was a pocket
of loose change.

Revelation

Suppose the past could not be recalled
any more than we can foretell
the future, that in order to remember
we'd have to visit an oracle,
or a storefront gypsy reading Tarot,
or consult astrologers
who could, so to speak, forecast history
by the alignment of stars.

There'd be no photographs,
but foreign grandmothers could recapture
our childhoods by reading the wrinkles
in tea bags. At a singles bar,
some after-work seeress might take our hands
and trace the lines of our palms
back to our first love affairs.

At such moments, the past
would suddenly bloom into consciousness
with a shock like clairvoyance.
What *had* happened would seem to loom
with the mystery of what *will* happen,
and stunned by this unwanted gift, we'd pray
for the revelation to be lifted.

For such visions become blinding.
Citizens of the shattered, ordinary order
would find themselves struggling to survive,
strung out somewhere between amnesia
and a paralyzing nostalgia, while those
most gifted with the second sight of memory
would wander honored, feared, and reviled,
as prophets wander through our present world.

Anti-Memoir

If there is any substitute for love
it's memory. —Joseph Brodsky

1

This is a street whose name and numbers
have been erased, although at dusk
smoke from its chimneys still hovers
as filmy as black lingerie.
This is a street to which love letters
addressed in the illegible smudge
of Ash Wednesday are delivered,
a street to which amnesiacs retire
to pen their memoirs, where autobiographies
are written in the third person,
and photographers erect their tripods
beneath black cloaks, then vanish
in a puff of light. This is a street
you can't step into twice,
it trails like footprints in snow
or, on a summer night,
appears suddenly, a run in a nylon.

2

A street without trees, without seasons.
(From where do the leaves come
that tumble in the wake of newspaper
raked by a Cyclone fence?) Autumn
of flying paper: moments torn
from diaries whirl through portals
left standing above plots of leveled bricks;
charred doorposts frame icons
who wander from niche to niche;
tattered topcoats draft down alleys,
drawn to the monument of fire
erected to those without a history.
There's an audible friction of shadows
slithering walls, susurrations,
as if in backlit rooms starched clothes
were being stripped from silhouettes.
In such a season it's easy to mistake
the watery reflections on shop windows
for a symptom of the body's gradual
dematerialization, when actually it's the soul
growing increasingly corporeal.

3

On this street, nakedness is measured
in discarded documents—expired passports,
delinquent bills, unredeemed pawn tickets—
relics of identity from the lull
before that first, seemingly innocent
notation—long since blown away—a blue
ballpoint's unmistakable scrawl
on a cocktail napkin from a seaside bar,
that read, *a freshly ironed blue sky*,
but meant instead to say, *the hot smell*
of her in my car, thighs
scorched against turquoise vinyl.
A cinnamon-smeared bakery bag,
on which *a scarred skating rink ghosts*
above a summer afternoon—daylight moon
that, decoded, may still be waiting
for *a night that rearranged*
the mnemonic structure of the heart,
or later, penciled like music
along the staff of a foreign postmark,
a dated word: *betrayed* . . . what or whom,
others or oneself, left unsaid.

4

At this hour, grated pawnshops appear
to jail all the lovely instruments
condemned to exile by electric guitars.
Along this block of lyres for sale,
the singing head is junked
as if it were an antiquated radio.
Follow the street singer, mute and blind,
he won't look back a second time.
Here, virgins abandon their illegitimates,
and magdalenes, whose stiletto
heels on concrete mimic the obsolete
lonely peck of a typewriter,
hang bedsheets to bleach back
to a tabula rasa, vast pages
blank as shrouds scribbled
with the automatic writing of wind.

5

The walls are a journal kept by crowds
passing into a phantasmagoric mural,
graphite coats the tablets of tenements
with the scorched patina of angels
in Prague, manholes vent
the illusion of heat at the core
of every spiritual world.
In noirish fog lit by a sparking tram,
the slumlord of the Tower of Babel
absconds with the rent.
This is a street whose tentacles
ravel about you, drawing you in,
la calle en su tinta,
a street stewed in its own ink.
Late for a dinner date, the disciple
corners his reflection on the window
of a bar, and stops to tie his noose
into a Windsor knot.

6

Tonight, follow the mute street singer.
Unimpeded by sight, he leads
down passageways you thought deleted,
diction stripped like stolen cars,
barricades of syntax broken by emotion,
sighs of plaster dust, the haze
of white space between words. Don't pause
for punctuation, here, a comma
of indecision elides into a coma,
and, years later, one wakes
to the interminable typing of rain
in a hotel where transients waste
money good for alcohol's blue flame
on sleep. Outside, the homeless
congregate while you continue to rent
all the rooms you've left behind,
addresses one must be lost to find,
knee-deep in flooded storm drains
clogged with crushed revisions,
a shredded blizzard, a ticker tape parade
gusting from the out-turned pockets
of the dead, enough litter
to trash the future, fuel without heat,
and yet, the past combustible enough
to be compressed into a fistful of soot.

7

Bell at an hour too late for the Angelus,
abandoned shop front with its flaking acronym:
MEAT, boarded shoe store where your foot size
is of interest to the Grand Inquisitor,
intersection where desire crossed
into obsession. To proceed further—
step by step, word by word—requires
a map of where *not* to go: avoid
the linearity of narrative, its illusion
of cause and effect, the chronology
of retrospect—a synonym for fate—
avoid the viaduct from which dice roll,
ghetto games of shells and shills,
the cardsharps cheating at Tarot.
Avoid the past tense of the oracle,
the politics of mediums—reactionary
dictates from their silent majority,
the dead—the current plague of angels,
the collectivization of the unconscious,
the monopoly on memory controlled
by ancestors posing as Poor Souls
who promise as inheritance
the status of a victim.

8

A bell too late for evening vespers
resonates through dark matter, flights
of lacunae limned in street light
migrate from the rookeries of a parish
that would vanish rather than undergo
an urban renewal of recollection.
From a hydrant, the Lethe leaks
into gutters where neon fish
feed on the reflections of meteors
rising back to heaven. The past
defying its own gravity,
leaving the present with the cry
within a song—a *hey!* . . . *aye!* . . . *olé!*—
the duende of a single nighthawk
reciting an anti-memoir,
a testament that takes the fifth
amendment of sleep, a nocturnal
history that renounces duration,
in which memory, more mysterious
and elusive than dream,
is conveyed in sign for fear
the future may overhear.

9

Daybook of a somnambulist, prayer
that precedes recorded time, oral tradition
preserved on illiterate backstreets
where street signs rhyme,
and the confessional of the last
pay phone rings. Answer,
and a stranger's voice reveals secrets
you've mistaken for identity,
your uncompleted story told
in a prose for listing groceries—
the unremembered, unredeemed,
ordinary, neither true nor false,
and unaccountable as love.
Above a flickered corner bulb,
the symbol of the nighthawk flares
into silence impossible to write.
Alone, along a street that's suddenly
like any other, you're blessed
simply to continue
another night's walk home.

ACKNOWLEDGMENTS

I wish to thank the editors of the magazines in which these poems appeared:

The American Poetry Review: "Three Nocturnes"

Another Chicago Magazine: "Maja"

Boulevard: "Ginny's Basement," "Revelation"

DoubleTake: "The Volcano"

Harvard Review: "Christening"

The Iowa Review: "Sirens"

Manoa: "Seven Sentences"

Meridian: "The Sunken Garden"

The Minnesota Review: "Three Windows"

The Missouri Review: "Benediction"

The New Republic: "Election Day"

Ontario Review: "Bath," "Current," "Narcissus," "*Shoesa*"

Poésie/première: "Chord"

Poetry: "Angelus," "Autobiography," "Chord," "Boundary," "Kitty-Corner," "Night Walk," "Swan," "Vigil"

Poetry Daily: "Vigil"

Poetry International: "Windy City"

Quarterly West: "View"

Skywriting: "Curtains," "Three Windows"

Tin House: "Journal"

TriQuarterly: "Anti-Memoir," "Mowing," "Vespers"

The Virginia Quarterly Review: "The Estrangement of Luis Leon," "Sleepers"

Westigan Review: "Curtains"

Witness: "Fish Camp," "Nylon"

Thanks also to the editors of the anthologies in which some of these poems have been reprinted:

American Diaspora: Poetry of Displacement. Virgil Suárez and Ryan G. Van Cleave, editors. University of Iowa Press, 2001.

The Best American Poetry 2003. Yusef Komunyakaa, guest editor; David Lehman, series editor. Scribner, 2003.

Contemporary American Poetry: Behind the Scenes. Ryan G. Van Cleave, editor. Allyn & Bacon / Longman, 2002.

Contemporary Michigan Poetry. Michael Delp, Conrad Hilberry, and Herbert Scott, editors. Wayne State University Press, 1988.

Illinois Voices. Kevin Stein and G. E. Murray, editors. University of Illinois Press, 2001.

Like Thunder: Poets Respond to Violence in America. Virgil Suárez and Ryan G. Van Cleave, editors. University of Iowa Press, 2002.

Poets of the New Century. Roger Weingarten and Richard Higgerson, editors. David R. Godine, 2001.

Urban Nature. Laura-Anne Bosselaar, editor. Milkweed Editions, 2000.